THE
LEADERSHIP
MINDSET

THE
LEADERSHIP
MINDSET

How Today's Successful Business Leaders Think

JOE CALLOWAY

Cover and text design by Sheila Parr
Cover image © Radachynskyi Serhii / Shutterstock

Cataloging-in-Publication data is available.
Print ISBN: 978-1-7328673-0-7
Printed in the United States of America
First Edition

To my friends John Bledsoe, Scott McKain,
Randy Pennington, Mark Sanborn, and Larry Winget.
It's a rare thing.

CONTENTS

THE
LEADERSHIP
MINDSET

The single most important factor in determining the success or failure of a business is the mindset of its leaders. It's how they think that makes the difference.

This isn't just what I believe to be true. This is what I know to be true. I know it because the reality of the marketplace tells me so.

Let me tell you what I've learned.

TODAY'S SUCCESSFUL LEADERS

Why does the title of this book say "today's" successful leaders? Has something about leadership changed lately?

Oh, yeah. You bet it has.

I've spent my entire career working with business leaders. They are my clients, my students, and always my teachers. I've worked with hundreds of companies of every size and in every business and endeavor you can think of. It has been my great opportunity to observe, work with, and learn from Fortune 500 CEOs, owners of small and midsized businesses, and young entrepreneurs launching start-ups. I've worked with leadership teams at companies that were riding waves of success and dominating their markets. I've also worked with leaders of companies that were struggling or even in full-blown crisis survival mode.

What it takes to succeed as a leader has most definitely changed, especially over just the past few years. I've had a front row seat in experiencing these changes while working with the top executives of some of the country's leading corporate giants as they confront disruption in their industries. Some were undergoing the challenging process of moving from sustaining the success of the present to redefining and reinventing themselves for the future.

As the Executive-in-Residence for Belmont University's Center For Entrepreneurship, I worked closely with students who were launching new businesses, often doing things that had never been done before. I'm an investor in and advisor to startups with dynamic young leaders who bring new approaches to organizational success. What's fascinating and significant is that the leadership mindset of a successful 22-year-old entrepreneur and that of a successful 62-year-old CEO of a big company are strikingly similar. Their thinking is quite a contrast to the mindset of the leaders with whom I worked a couple of decades ago. It has to be.

One of my personal mantras is, "If you're successful, you know what *used* to work." The idea is that my success has been in markets that no longer exist, because markets change continuously. If I do what I've always done, I won't get what I've always gotten. Instead, I'll go out of business. The leadership mindset has to not only respond to change, but also be the driver of it.

Any of us could make a list of dozens of characteristics that go into effective leadership. This book is about a few that I believe are critically important, especially in today's marketplace. They are among the common threads woven through the thinking of the best leaders that I know. My intention is for this book to give you some new perspectives on leadership that can be of value in how you think about your own role and responsibilities as a leader.

Your mindset is what empowers and even inspires you and your people to sustain and continue to grow the success you've already created, while at the same time discovering and implementing the new ideas for what your business must become to ensure your success going forward. No two successful leaders think exactly alike, but there are some easily identifiable things that most great leaders have in common. This is where leadership starts: with mindset.

LEAD WITH INTENTION

I've known some people in leadership positions who almost seemed like they were starting over every day. They had no real clarity on a guiding purpose. They went to work with a defensive attitude and always projected the sense that something was wrong. Decisions were situational, reactive, and without consistency. Their colleagues and employees felt unsure about what to do because there were too many so-called priorities, and any idea of what mattered most was a moving target.

Rather than inspire confidence, these leaders created a culture of blame, finger-pointing and second-guessing. There was little or no mutual trust, which inevitably created an "every man for himself" culture. Nobody felt like anyone had their back, least of all their leader.

Successful and effective leadership is intentional.

An effective leader makes decisions and takes action *on* purpose and *with* purpose. Decisions and actions are aligned with the values and culture of the organization and serve to advance the strategy and ultimately achieve the organization's purpose, which is clearly understood by every employee. Intentional leadership means that things don't happen by chance, but rather by design.

Thinking of the successful, inspiring, and truly effective leaders that I've known and worked with in my career, I always had the very strong sense that their decisions, large or small, were driven by clear and steady intention. That applied to everything from strategy to how they interacted with employees.

One company that stands out in my mind as having leadership that is very intentional is Journeys, a national footwear retailer. What impresses me so much about the leadership team at Journeys is that they work hard to get clarity about intention and purpose at all levels of the company. In their in-house leadership training there is great emphasis on the "why" behind everything that they do.

Being intentional is no guarantee that you'll always make the right decision. Indeed, all great leaders sometimes take risks and sometimes make mistakes. But they have clarity on the *why* behind decisions and they can change direction when necessary without any sense of panic.

The intentional leader projects a continual sense of "I've got this. We've got this. We know what we're doing and why we're doing it."

When you lead with intention, it invites confidence.

When you lead with intention, it builds trust.

When you lead with intention, day in and day out, it inspires others to do the same.

Let acting with absolute intention, along with non-negotiable values of ethics, honesty, and trust be your foundation for leadership.

Asking The Tough Questions

- *I make decisions with clear thought and absolute intention. Yes/No*
- *I have clarity on the reason and purpose behind every decision I make. Yes/No*
- *Through my actions and communication as a leader, my employees and colleagues know that I am intentional in what I do. Yes/No*
- *What is the first step I will take in being more intentional?*
- *How will I teach the discipline and mindset of being intentional to others?*
- *What will I build into my daily activities that will help me be intentional?*

LEADERS SIMPLIFY THE COMPLICATED

I believe that one of a leader's core responsibilities is to simplify the complicated. You should seek out and destroy complication anywhere it exists. "Complicated" is the enemy of everything that you are trying to accomplish. "Making it simple" should be such an ingrained way of doing things that you make it part of the way you think and an underlying principle in your company's culture.

In my leadership workshops I say, "Raise your hand if you frequently have this thought: 'We're making this way more complicated than it needs to be.'" Without fail, every hand in the room goes up. So what's up with that? Why do we overthink, over-plan and overcomplicate our businesses? Because it's easy. Because any knucklehead can make something complicated. It almost seems to be imbedded in our DNA. As Warren Buffet said, "There seems to be some perverse human characteristic that likes to make easy things difficult."

The more complicated you've made your business, the less effective you'll be. Complication freezes you into uncertainty and inaction. Simplicity enables you to create clarity, which lets you get yourself and everyone else focused on shared visions, goals, and priorities. It's extremely hard for anyone, much less an entire organization, to focus on anything that's complicated.

Making things complicated is easy, and it gets in our way. It's an obstacle of our own making. Making things simple, on the other hand, is hard, but it is one of the keys to success. To simplify takes intelligence, patience, and a keen insight into how things and people work. We have to fight against our seemingly natural inclination to add more and, instead, follow the philosophy of Antoine de Saint-Exupéry, who said, "Perfection is achieved, not when there is nothing more to add, but when there is nothing left to take away."

I wrote a book called *Keep It Simple* that has done surprisingly well. I say "surprisingly" because I didn't anticipate the demand for such a simple message about simplicity itself. The biggest fans of the book tend to be experienced business leaders. Since the book came out I have been hired by a number of companies to do leadership development work with them, and their only connection to me was that the CEO or some other leader had read *Keep It Simple.* To this day, simplicity is one of the key concepts in my leadership development work. People are hungry for it. Effective leaders understand that they have to master it.

Think of your own business. What might be the return to and impact on your bottom line if every facet of your business was made simpler? Think of customer touch points, internal processes, communication, strategy, tactics—everything! When you simplify, you empower yourself, your people, and your business.

You may be in a business that is, by nature, extremely complicated. If that's true, then the need for you to simplify everything possible is even more important. Your success may in part depend on your value proposition being that you simplify the complicated for the customer. Ultimately, it all goes back to your ability to simplify.

One of my clients is a major US defense contractor. Trust me when I tell you that the products they develop for our government are very, very complicated. I did a workshop with about 300 members of their leadership team, most of whom were engineers and scientists. Their response to the "simplify everything possible" message was enthusiastic. One senior VP wrote me afterwards, saying, "We're discovering that simplifying everything possible helps us add value to all that we do."

Another group that I worked with on the simplicity mindset was a leadership retreat with the 60 top executives for a national commercial construction company. About a month after the retreat, the CEO told me, "We usually come back from this retreat with a list of 70 or 80 things that we want to do. We seldom follow through very well on any of them. You sent us back with a list that we each developed of three things that we need to get right every single day. It has made a world of difference."

All of this begs the question, "As a leader, exactly what should I seek to simplify?" The answer is, "Everything." For me, it ranges from my communication with clients and colleagues, to our website, to the actual leadership workshops that I develop and deliver. It's everything. You should declare war on anything more complicated than it needs to be.

If you and your team set out on a mission to simplify and you empower your people to make it so, you will be astounded at the positive impact it will have on your performance and results. A bonus is the impact on employee morale. Taking a business from complicated to simple can do more to boost the spirits of employees than a thousand pizza parties could ever do.

Asking The Tough Questions

- *I do a great job of simplifying the complicated for myself and for the team. Yes/No*
- *What do I need to simplify first?*
- *What are the things we need to simplify?*
- *With customers?*
- *Internally?*
- *With vendors and partners?*
- *With our communication?*
- *With our values, mission, purpose, or goals?*
- *What else do we need to simplify?*
- *Who will be responsible for it?*
- *How will they be empowered?*
- *What is our timetable for it?*

LEADERS CREATE
CLARITY

When you simplify, you get clarity. With clarity, everyone has a shared understanding of what's going on and what matters most. If you then become the best at what matters most, you win. Period. It's how the market works.

I want to focus on one aspect of how a leader effectively clarifies, and that is through brevity. As I write this chapter, I see the irony in writing a few hundred words to address the concept of clarity through brevity. But it's a book, not a purpose statement, and I look at this as a conversation. I want to present the concept of clarity through brevity from a number of perspectives, so I allow myself the luxury of some time and space and words to do so. A successful leader does the same thing, making a simply worded concept clear through the ongoing reinforcement of it. The concept itself, though, should be as concisely worded as possible.

Some leaders fall into the trap of thinking that the more complicated an idea is and the more words it takes to express it, the more impressive or impactful it is. In fact, quite the opposite is true. The leadership mindset always strives for clarity, which usually goes hand in hand with brevity. Whether it's your vision, your mission, or your goals for the year, try and make it 20 words or less. As Albert Einstein said, "If you can't explain it simply, you don't understand it well enough." What I have learned for sure is that the more plainly spoken and clearly defined your message is, the greater its effectiveness.

There's a classic story with many versions that are attributed to a variety of people. The most popular and oft-quoted version is about President Woodrow Wilson.

"How long does it take you to prepare one of your speeches?" asked a friend of President Wilson. "That depends on the length of the speech," answered the President. "If it is a 10-minute speech, it takes me all of two weeks to prepare it; if it is a half-hour speech, it takes me a week; if I can talk as long as I want to, it requires no preparation at all. I am ready now."

Just as it takes no particular wisdom or skill to make things complicated, the same is true for giving a long speech or writing an unnecessarily long report.

Anybody can rattle on forever. To be concise; to be clear—that takes talent.

In business, I often see mission, vision, or value statements so wordy and full of "corporate-speak" that they cease to have any real meaning to anyone. I did consulting work with an medical emergency treatment company. At one of their leadership events, the CEO had the company's three-paragraph mission statement on a screen to read aloud to the group so that everyone "is clear on what we're all about."

When I spoke to the group later in the day, I asked if anyone could summarize their mission statement into just one sentence. No one volunteered, so I picked one woman in the audience and kept asking her to try until, with an obvious sense of frustration, she finally blurted out, "Look, we help people when they're hurt, okay?"

Okay, indeed. Her statement is exactly the kind of clarity that you want to achieve. I asked the group how many of them got out of bed every morning thinking about, excited about, and committed to achieving their three-paragraph mission statement. None of them raised their hands, including the CEO. I asked how many of them could be excited about "helping people when they're hurt." Every hand in the room went up. There's the purpose: "we help people when they're hurt." The power and effectiveness of such clarity is two-fold:

1. It's easy to understand.

2. It engages people on an emotional level.

As of this writing, Mary Barra is the CEO of GM. In 2009, when Barra had been vice president of global human resources, she went to war on bureaucracy, which she felt was holding back the potential of the organization. GM's company dress code was a perfect example. It was pages upon pages of specific directions of how people in different jobs should dress for different situations.

Barra changed the multi-page dress code to two words, "Dress appropriately." Of course there was pushback from managers who said that people would misinterpret, that there would be differences of opinions on what "appropriately" means, etc. Barra told the managers that it was their job to talk with their people about it. So they did, and guess what—the dress code works.

I don't share this to get you to change your dress code. I share it to show you that this kind of communication is powerful and it's effective, and to illustrate how impactful the right few words can be in achieving clarity.

Some leaders resist plain speaking because "we want it to sound professional." Wordiness doesn't make something professional. If it's so wordy that you don't reach people both intellectually and emotionally, if they don't "get it" on a gut level, then it won't work. If it doesn't work, *that's* unprofessional.

Don't misunderstand my point. You can't just come up with a three-word clever slogan and necessarily expect that it delivers clarity. The test is whether or not people truly do "get it." The fact is that people, meaning employees and customers in this context, tend to more clearly understand something said with brevity than they do something said with verbosity.

It's true with the expression of any idea. As an investor, if an entrepreneur says to me, "Let me explain my idea for this business. It's kind of complicated," I'm out. They lost me at hello. If your explanation to me is complicated, then how will the market and potential customers be able to understand it?

I'm an investor in and advisor to startups that were founded by brilliant young entrepreneurs. I wrote the checks to invest in Gilson Snow and in EVAmore because I believed in both the people and in the concepts.

Nick Gilson explained his snowboard company by saying that their unique design enabled any rider to do more and have more fun with the snowboard. Simple. Channing Moreland and Makenzie Stokel of EVAmore told me that their online company made it easier to book bands for events. Simple. In the cases of both companies, their leaders expressed ideas with clarity.

I can't invest in it, believe in it, commit to it, be motivated by it, get excited about it, or feel much of anything about it if there's a lack of clarity. Today's successful leaders, like Nick, Channing, and Makenzie, are masters of clarity. Their communication is direct, effective, and what I think of as being "clean." When they speak or write, you understand exactly what they mean.

I spent three days acting as "the outside perspective" at a retreat with the leadership team of a nonprofit agency that serves the needs of young women. One of their challenges was that they knew that they needed greater clarity on their purpose. They had a very long statement of purpose that they agreed didn't give them or their teams a good sense of what the point of it all was, nor did it particularly inspire anyone to action.

We went to work and they ultimately boiled their lengthy statement of purpose down to three words.

Those three words defined who they wanted to be, the work that they wanted to do, and was deeply inspiring and motivating to everyone in the group. The three words? "We empower girls."

Six months later the CEO told me that coming up with those three words was one of the hardest exercises they had ever been through and was possibly the single most important leadership decision and action they had ever taken as a group. They felt focused, intentional, and inspired by their new three-word statement of purpose.

It's not just about emotional commitment. It's also about day-to-day organizational effectiveness. When your people don't have clarity on what's important or what's expected, they muddle through their day. They can't be productive if they are unclear about what they're working for or what their work means. They also can't prioritize their workload effectively, meaning that projects and tasks get completed in the wrong order.

Creating clarity takes insight, the skill of communicating well, and, most of all, your own complete understanding of exactly what it is that you're trying to say. The leadership mindset always asks, "Is this absolutely crystal clear? Is there any chance for misunderstanding? Will everyone 'get it'"?

Asking The Tough Questions

- *Everyone in our organization has absolute clarity about our purpose. Yes/No*

- *I have done an excellent job of expressing myself with clarity. Yes/No*

- *Where would greater clarity create better results for our business?*

- *What will I do immediately to achieve greater clarity in my communication?*

- *What will we do to achieve clarity in communication throughout the organization?*

- *Who are the people in the organization that can best help us create clarity?*

LEADERS CREATE
FOCUS

Sir Peter Blake led Team New Zealand to successive victories in the America's Cup yacht competition in 1995 and 2000. One key to their success was that Blake focused the team on one question. The question was simply this: "Will it make the boat go faster?"

Every thing that they did and every decision that they made had to go through the filter of "Will it make the boat go faster?" This applied to the equipment that they chose, their training regimen, nutrition, crew composition—everything.

The British eight man rowing team in the 2000 Sydney Olympics adopted the same strategy of "Will it make the boat go faster?" and it drove them to change everything about their strategy and daily activities. They credit this singular focus with their winning the gold medal. I highly recommend the book about this team and their leadership mindset, *Will It Make the Boat Go Faster?*, by Ben Hunt-Davis.

We can all focus more effectively using that same question. We all have a "boat" that we want to go faster. Look at your daily choices, activities, and decisions and ask yourself your own version of "Will this make the boat go faster?"

Consider the sheer power and irresistible force of a team, whether five people or five thousand, in which every member shares the same singular focus. Then the members individually bring their own sets of skills to their own particular jobs in order to achieve the shared goal. With that focus, you become almost undefeatable. Without focus, it's difficult to accomplish much of anything.

Focus also keeps you from falling into the trap of "and you know what else we could do?" Drive and ambition can cause any of us to fall in love with the next idea. I am Exhibit A. I will be working on what I know is essential for my business to succeed, then become distracted by the next, new, shiny idea. One essential function of focus is to help us tell the difference between opportunities and distractions.

A leader who isn't focused will have an organization in disarray. Without focus, all of your mission, vision, and strategy statements become nothing more than exercises in wishful thinking. As a leader you must *be* focused and you must *create* focus.

Asking The Tough Questions

- *I am focused on what matters most. Yes/No*
- *My focus drives my daily actions and decisions. Yes/No*
- *I lead my team in being and staying focused. Yes/No*
- *We consistently focus on high-return activities. Yes/No*
- *What will I do today to bring more focus to my thinking and my work?*
- *How do I define "making our boat go faster?"*
- *What should "Will it make the boat go faster!" mean to me?*
- *What should it mean to the team?*
- *What will I do today to ensure that I will consistently focus on high-return activities?*
- *What will I do today to ensure that the team will consistently focus on high-return activities?*

LEADERS
MAKE IT EASY

Making things easy is a leader's companion piece to making things simple. As with simplification, the answer to the question "What should I do to make easy?" is, "Everything."

I'll give you some of your end-of-the-chapter questions in advance:

Do we make it easy for people to do their best at their jobs?

How can we make it easier?

Do we make it easy for customers to do business with us?

How can we make it easier?

Do we make it easy for customers to give us truly useful feedback?

How can we make it easier?

Do we make it easy for employees to give us truly useful feedback?

How can we make it easier?

Do we make our product or service easy to buy?

How can we make it easier?

Do we make our product or service easy to access, understand, and use?

How can we make it easier?

Do we make our product or service easy to recommend?

How can we make it easier?

You can apply the "is it easy?" and the "how can we make it easier?" questions to almost every facet of your business, and you should.

As the leader of a business endeavor, you are ultimately responsible for your organization's ability to acquire and keep customers, which many would say is the fundamental reason that any business exists. Ask yourself this question:

Would it be a powerful competitive advantage if we were considered the easiest to do business with in our market?

Allow me to answer. "Yes!" Being the easiest to do business with is the mother lode in terms of being a decisive differentiator to today's buyer of absolutely anything—from accounting services or concert tickets to cars, shoe repairs, banking, haircuts, or commercial aircraft. When you reduce the effort required by a customer you automatically add value.

Consider companies often cited as disruptors: companies that everyone is talking about. What makes them so popular?

- Uber/Lyft: make it easier to catch a ride.
- Amazon Prime: makes it incredibly easy to buy anything.
- Apple: products that are easy to use.
- Google: makes it easier to use the internet.
- Zappos: makes ordering, returns, and customer service extremely easy.

Your favorite apps on your smartphone: all of them make something easier.

About once a year, I tear down my website and rebuild it with the main goal being to make it simpler and easier to use. If I do that, then I've succeeded in advancing my strategy in one of the most effective ways possible. I always try and apply the standard of "make it easier" to everything I do in my business.

If you are intentionally leading your organization in an effort to make things easier to understand, access, use, or buy, then you're succeeding at one of your most important jobs.

Asking The Tough Questions

- *I make difficult things easier. Yes/No*
- *What are the areas in our business in which we need to make things easier?*
- *What are the steps that we will take immediately to begin that process?*

CULTURE:
YOUR GREATEST
COMPETITIVE
ADVANTAGE

It has been said that a manager's job is to be sure that the organization is functioning as it is designed to, and that a leader's job is to remind everyone of "who we are." Culture is who you are expressed through how you behave with each other and everyone else. Culture is your shared values. It's both the foundation and a set of guidelines for everything that you do. If you get your culture right, meaning that if everyone is in alignment and intentional about upholding your values, you significantly increase your odds of success. If you don't get culture right, then it's not going to work. Your culture can be your greatest competitive advantage, or it can be an obstacle that is always in your way.

You can't *not* have a culture. The question is whether your culture is intentional and by design, or whether it simply emerged with no rhyme or reason, tends to be situational, and is purely defined by the behavior of the strongest personalities in the organization. But rest assured, you have a culture. Does it work to advance your strategy and your cause in the interest of your ultimate purpose, or does it get in your way?

As the leader, you are the prime keeper and defender of the culture. It is your job. While everyone is part of the culture, you can't delegate this one, because you are the embodiment of the culture. Regardless of what it says on the poster in the break room about "Our Culture," everyone looks to you, what you say, and, more important, how you behave to know what the organization stands for.

The best guideline I know for defining culture is that it is "who we are."

A very successful and effective senior executive for a telecommunications company once told me that he learned the importance of culture from his father, who had one simple and focused message for his children, which he repeated over and over: "Remember who you are."

He said that his father often talked about the

values that were important in their family. The values were things like honesty, generosity, courage, and being ladies and gentlemen. These were the values that made them who they were as a family.

The executive told me that as a teenager, when he would go out on Saturday night with his friends, his father would say to him, "Have a great time tonight, and remember who you are." That's all he had to say to remind his son to make good decisions.

What a simple, powerful lesson for a family or for any organization. When making decisions of any kind, or when we face changes or challenges, we can stay on course with our values if we just go by the guidance of "Remember who you are."

Culture only works to your advantage if it is lived by everyone in the organization and made real by the leadership. Let's look at some examples of effective cultures that are brought to life by effective leaders.

One of my clients was a bank that had a culture value that stated simply, "We are a team." I attended a reception the bank was hosting for its biggest commercial customers. Attending the reception from the bank were senior executives and a range of employees. I was with the CEO of the bank when he introduced one of the tellers to an executive from a customer company. The CEO didn't say, "I'd like you to meet

Linda, a teller at the bank." Instead, he said, "I'd like you to meet Linda, one of my colleagues at the bank."

"One of my colleagues." By putting it that way, the CEO expressed a level of respect for that employee as his fellow team member. That was who the CEO was. He felt that all of the bank's employees were vitally important members of the team, and he treated them that way. Not surprisingly, that was the model of behavior that everyone followed.

I was the main speaker at an annual leadership meeting for 500 store managers and assistant managers for a large midwestern grocery store chain. At one point in the meeting morning I noticed about ten guys enter the meeting room with who I guessed to be their wives. They stood at the back of the room, seemingly nervous and looking uncomfortable in their suits and ties. These were working guys, not executives. You could just tell.

Before the break for lunch, the CEO took the stage and said "And now we come to the most important part of this meeting. Could I have you gentlemen in the back come up on the stage? And please have your wives come up, too." The vibe in the room got very serious as the group made their way up onto the stage. I could tell that something important was taking place, but at that point I didn't know what.

The CEO continued by saying, "We all know that the number-one value in our culture is that we care about people. We care about customers, we care about our communities, and we certainly care about each other. There is nothing more important than our people and their families. That's why throughout the history of this company we have made safety our top priority. It's more important than sales or profits or anything else. Today, as we do each year, we honor our truck drivers with the best safety records for upholding that value of people and safety. Nothing we do as a company means more than these men doing their jobs professionally and with utmost safety for themselves and others."

As someone removed a cloth covering from a table of plaques and envelopes, the CEO went on. "It is my great honor to present each of you with our highest honor. This plaque honors your commitment to our value of safety and caring about people, and with it I also present each of you with a check in appreciation to you for who you are and what you do. You remind us daily of what matters most. We also are honored to have your wives here with you. None of us can succeed without the support of others, and we recognize the important roles that you, the families of our best people, play in their success." With that, the

CEO presented each truck driver with a plaque and a check and congratulated the wives, as well.

As this was happening, the 500 store managers and assistant managers stood together and gave those truck drivers one of the most enthusiastic, sustained, and sincere standing ovations I have ever seen.

This was a celebration and reinforcement of culture through ceremony, ritual, and recognition. Culture isn't just an intellectual exercise. If I believe it and know it in my head, that's one thing. But if I believe it and know it in my heart, that's quite another, and much more powerful. It's a good and constructive thing to get emotional about what matters most. Great leaders know the cultural value of genuine goosebumps and even occasional tears.

I worked with the leadership team of a company that sold products direct to consumers via telephone and the internet. The company had about 20,000 employees, many of whom were involved in manufacturing and shipping. One of their culture values was: "Every job is mission critical."

I accompanied the CEO on a "walking around" tour of the company, which was something that he did on a regular basis, when he stopped to speak with a woman whose job was quality control. She checked each order to be sure that it had been filled correctly and to check the products for any possible defects. This was the last step in the process before shipping.

The CEO asked her how she felt about some recent changes that had been made in the vision and mission statements for the company. She said that they seemed fine to her, but that her job didn't really have much connection to all of that.

The CEO seized on that opportunity to assure the woman that not only was her job connected to the company's vision and mission, but that it was critically important to their success. "You are the last stop between our product and our customer. You are our brand. If the order is done right, then you've made the brand shine. If it's wrong, then that's our brand to that customer. I'm not exaggerating one bit when I say that our reputation depends on your job."

The woman seemed to stand a little taller as she said, "Well, when you put it that way, I guess it is pretty important to the customer." The CEO responded by saying, "And it's vitally important to us. Thanks for doing what you do and doing it so well."

There are actually two contrasting lessons to be learned from that story. The good news is that the CEO took that obvious opportunity to engage with an employee and strengthen her connection with the company and its cultural value of "Every job is mission critical." The bad news is that the employee felt disconnected in the first place. What was going on with her supervisor? Why didn't that supervisor create the connection, protect the culture, and keep it going every single day?

Leaders too often mistakenly expect things to happen by memo, or meeting, or osmosis, instead of taking on the responsibility that things happen, good or bad, because of everyday, intentional leadership or the lack thereof. "Lead" is a verb.

At a meeting of five hundred sales reps for an airline, a series of executives spoke to the group about the state of the company, new initiatives, priorities for the coming year, etc. The last speaker of the morning was the national vice president of sales, and as he walked on stage he received an enthusiastic standing ovation from his employees.

He told them to sit and said that they might want to take that ovation back in a few minutes. He had nothing but tough news for them. It was a classic case of "you're going to have to do a lot more with fewer resources to work with." It was quite simply a hard time for the company and for sales in particular. The VP didn't pull any punches, didn't try to sugarcoat anything, and he openly acknowledged the extreme difficulty of the challenge before them. He closed with words of encouragement and expressed his belief in them and his appreciation for all that they did. He left the stage to another, possibly even more enthusiastic, standing ovation.

It was a case of the obvious, but I had to ask. I talked with some of the sales reps as they left the auditorium on their way to lunch. I asked them why the VP got such an ovation after delivering nothing but really tough news. The answer was the same from everyone. They said that the VP unconditionally respected every one of his employees, and that he was always completely honest and transparent with them about what was going on. They always knew where they stood with him.

In return, they said that he expected them to be respectful of each other and everyone else in the company, and to treat customers and vendors with that same level of respect. He also expected complete and total honesty from them. They said that they could tell or ask him anything.

In this company, at least with the employees of this VP of Sales, culture was very real. It was how they lived and worked together, day in and day out. Their culture of respect and honesty didn't have to be looked up in the company handbook. Everyone could see it playing out right in front of their eyes. That's leadership.

The vitally important point that I want to make here is that I've seen too many companies in which "culture" was a synonym for "poster on the wall." It was a list of qualities or attributes or feel-good thoughts written so leadership could check it off of their list of things to do. Their attitude seemed to be, "Culture? Oh sure. We've got it written down and we pull the poster out at a meeting every now and then."

Your culture is who you are. Your success or failure as an organization depends, in great part, on the strength of that culture. I go back to my original question, "Is your culture intentional and by design?"

Asking The Tough Questions

- *I am ultimately responsible for our culture. Yes/No*

- *(If "No," then who is?)*

- *We are completely intentional about our culture. Yes/No*

- *We have work to do on our culture. Yes/No*

CULTURE
DRIVES SUCCESS:
HUGHES MARINO

In this book I don't reference many companies by name, so it's a bold statement on my part to single out a company for its culture. I've worked with hundreds of companies and their leadership teams over the course of my career. I've seen the best of the best and I'm not easily impressed. When it comes to a culture that drives extraordinary results, there is one company that I absolutely respect and admire. I offer them as a model for how it can be done.

Hughes Marino is an award-winning commercial real estate firm exclusively representing tenants and buyers. They are located in San Diego, Seattle, Los Angeles, and other West Coast cities, plus an office in New York. To say that Hughes Marino is a successful company and market leader is quite the understatement.

Hughes Marino has an incredibly talented and motivated team who are among the very best in the world at what they do. I have spent enough time with the company to have some insight into what creates and sustains their remarkable success. While acknowledging the vital role of their talent, skill, and drive, I would credit their success primarily to leadership and culture.

On the company website, they put it this way: "We believe that an organization's success is about so much more than hard work. It's about cultivating a compelling culture. It's about investing in people. It's about embracing the family spirit. At Hughes Marino, we're one big family, working together and motivating each other towards our shared and individual goals. We hope that the first thing you notice when you step foot through our front doors is the welcoming and supportive environment that we've worked so hard to create."

I believe that culture is Hughes Marino's greatest differentiator. It's their culture that makes the people there love to go to work, and that is the most powerful competitive advantage you can have. It's a great place to work, and that's not just my opinion.

Here is some of the recognition that Hughes Marino has received:

#1 Best Small Workplace in the Nation—
Fortune Magazine

#3 Top Company Culture in the Nation
(Medium Companies Division) | 2017—
Entrepreneur

#2 Top Company Culture in the Nation
(Small Companies Division)
2015 & 2018—*Entrepreneur*

#4 Best Workplace in Southern California—
Fortune Magazine

Top 100 Best Workplaces for Millennials
in the Nation 2018—*Fortune Magazine*

Best Workplaces 2018—*Inc. Magazine*

#1 Best Place to Work in Los Angeles—
Los Angeles Business Journal

#1 Best Place to Work in Orange County—
Orange County Business Journal

#1 Best Place to Work in San Diego—
San Diego Business Journal

Washington's 100 Best Workplaces 2018—*Puget Sound Business Journal*

Best Commercial Real Estate Company (Multiple Years)—*Union Tribune*

Workplace Excellence Award Medallion Winner—Society for Human Resource Management

Most Admired Companies (Multiple Years)—*SD Metro Magazine*

Most Trusted Brand—*SD Metro Magazine*

None of this happens by accident. Go back to the first of the shared characteristic of successful leaders that opened the book: Lead with intention. That's what President & COO Shay Hughes, Chairman & CEO Jason Hughes, and the entire leadership team all do at Hughes Marino. Their intentions are guided by and their culture is based on their 10 core values. While theirs is a very numbers-intensive business, one thing that has always impressed me is that the numbers aren't usually what I hear Jason and Shay talking about. They are more likely to be talking about some aspect of their culture or their values. Those values are at the heart of who they are and what they do, day in and day out.

Here are the Hughes Marino core values:

1. Always do the right thing.

2. Deliver excellence in everything we do.

3. Enjoy the journey.

4. Embrace the family spirit.

5. Build lasting relationships.

6. Nurture your personal and professional life.

7. Pursue growth and learning.

8. Give generously to others.

9. Proactively communicate with everyone.

10. Be authentic, grateful, and humble.

These aren't slogans. These aren't for posters to decorate the walls. These values are who they are. It's in their DNA as an organization.

I talked with Shay Hughes about the impact that an intentional and vibrant culture based on a clear set of values has had on their business.

Joe: *How important has culture been to your success?*

Shay: Culture has been absolutely vital to our success. It has dramatically transformed our company as a standout in the highly competitive commercial real estate industry and also revolutionized how the industry will operate in the future. While most brokers compete against each other within their own company, our brokers and entire team of subject matter experts work together, in a collaborative, supportive, and non-competitive environment with unprecedented operational support. Our company is rapidly expanding across the United States, with top-grossing brokers reaching out to us on a regular basis wanting to join Hughes Marino, to be a part of a company that is taking tenant representation to the next level. Not only do we provide a unique service by only representing commercial tenants, we operate ethically and with integrity, keen attention to detail, respect, and authenticity. While we provide an incredible service experience and outcome for our clients (we even guarantee it, which is unheard of in our industry), many companies are eager to work with us solely because of our ten core values, nationally recognized culture, and how we treat our team.

Joe: *You're growing rapidly. How do you keep culture healthy when integrating a new business into Hughes Marino?*

Shay: A perfect example of our growth through the influence of our award-winning culture is our Seattle office. When two brokers from one of the largest commercial real estate firms in the world came to us to propose Hughes Marino Seattle, we knew we were onto something. It was a big step, but it paid off tremendously, and we were even named the #1 Best Workplace in Washington in the Small/Medium Business category the first year of operation. That was the cherry on top of a fantastic decision, and that initiative led us to expand nationally at our clients' request. As such, more leaders came to us, intrigued by our culture and with interest in joining Hughes Marino.

Joe: *What do you do to keep the culture alive and well?*

Shay: Maintaining our tight-knit culture begins with hiring the right team members. No matter how much we need to fill a new position or how long it takes to find that right candidate, we never compromise on hiring. During the interview process, we look for people who embody our core values and have stand-out, high moral character, who will fit right in with our friendly and outgoing team. Once we find that person, we welcome them to our family and make sure it is a top-notch experience so they know they are valued right off the bat!

We also heavily encourage appreciation and gratitude, and one of the most fulfilling ways we embrace appreciation is through our WOW cards. Each year our team members are given five WOW cards worth $50, to present to their peers during team meetings for going above and beyond, both inside and out of work. Believe it or not, we have witnessed so many happy tears during our WOW card portion of our meetings, and the team leaves feeling uplifted by kind acts, positivity, and appreciation. We've found it is a wonderful way to genuinely bond and also encourages teammates to go out of their way to help both our clients and our team.

Another way Jason and I maintain our culture is through enriching the lives of our team in any way we can. Aside from the monthly birthday celebrations, billiards and shuffleboard tournaments held in our game rooms, and fun contests held across all offices, we bring in business coaches (including Joe!) to uplift and inspire our team. We also provide full healthcare benefits and student loan assistance and provide our team with a lot of extra time off around the holidays (in addition to vacation days) to be able to spend time with families and recharge.

We do everything in our power to make sure all of our amazing team members feel valued, fulfilled, and happy to come to work every day with people who care about each other like a family. And judging by the continuous local and national recognition we've been humbled to receive, our culture is alive and well!

Joe: *Why does culture really matter that much in a numbers-intensive business?*

Shay: It makes a dramatic difference. To have the opportunity to work amongst truly kind-hearted, driven, and intelligent people while revolutionizing the industry is a rewarding opportunity for all of us, Jason and myself included! Our company culture is what has attracted some of the most talented, sought-after candidates from across the country to Hughes Marino. Each team member has added so much to our company, from their cultural contributions to their talent, intelligence, and grit, all of which has played a major part in our success and national expansion. Our brokers are supported by the entire team: from our deep operational support to project and construction management, planning and design, culture consulting, lease audit and administration, and in-house legal team. This, in turn, helps them to be wildly successful, earning more than 27 times greater revenue than our competitors.

Another reason culture matters? It truly is a competitive advantage, drastically setting us apart from other commercial real estate firms. Companies come to us to utilize our expertise in order to enhance their own offices and company culture to attract top talent. Nothing is more rewarding than helping others succeed alongside us and positively impacting workplaces and people's lives every day!

Our emphasis on company culture has proven to be a game changer for our company, and we can't wait to see where this success takes us in the decades to come!

Joe: *Thanks, Shay.*

I'm not at all suggesting that your values or your culture should be the same as or even remotely resemble that of Hughes Marino, although they are a great model. What I am telling you with 100% certainty and intention on my part is that, as a leader, your job is to create clarity on what your culture is, and then nurture and protect it.

The reason that I'm singling out Hughes Marino is because they are such a great example for all of us. While it's certainly not easy, any company of any size in any business can do what they have done. It's the result of pure leadership and focus. Whether you are a one-person practice or a large corporation, you can make your culture your greatest competitive advantage.

For more insight and ideas about culture, I strongly encourage you to take a look at the Hughes Marino website and to pay particular attention to everything in the "About" section.

Go to: hughesmarino.com

For more on how leaders like those at Hughes Marino make culture real, check out the chapter "Leaders Repeat and Reinforce."

LEADERS KNOW WHAT'S GOING ON— WHAT'S *REALLY* GOING ON

When Ed Koch was mayor of New York, he was famous for asking people on the street, "How am I doing?" Effective leaders are comfortable asking that question, and they expect honest answers. They see themselves as being on a never-ending listening tour. They know that to make sound decisions they have to know what's going on. They have to have honest and accurate feedback from colleagues, employees, vendors, customers, potential customers, the marketplace, and the community at large.

In a TED Talk, Ray Dalio, author of the mega-successful book, *Principles: Life and Work*, tells a story of a really tough evaluation he received from an employee, Jim, about a presentation that Dalio had given in a meeting. In an email, the employee told Dalio that he deserved a "D-" for his lack of preparation and disorganization.

It's in Dalio's reaction to the brutally honest email that his depth of leadership comes through. In the TED Talk, Dalio says, "It's great because I need feedback like that. And it's great because if I don't let Jim and people like Jim express their points of view, our relationship wouldn't be the same."

I presented a series of leadership workshops with a group of executives from a number of different companies. In one of the workshops, we talked about the top mistakes that leaders make. As we discussed the mistakes, I had them do a self-assessment survey and rate themselves on how they felt they did on the issues, which included such things as being out of touch, letting momentum and enthusiasm fizzle, making things too complicated, etc.

One of the participants took the self-assessment a step further. He reworded the survey so that his senior management team could rate him. He gave the survey to each member of his team, told them to be completely honest in their ratings, and scheduled a meeting with them for the end of the day to discuss the results.

The young CEO said that it was the scariest thing he had ever done as a leader. He also said that it turned out to be one of the most productive and positive things he had ever done. The feedback was invaluable in helping him become more effective, and the positive impact on the company and its culture was considerable.

A leader has to constantly look for ways to grow and improve. You have to know "how you are doing" from the people on your team.

I am amazed at the number of people in senior leadership positions who don't know what's really going on in their organizations. They may know what the numbers tell them and they may read the reports and hear the updates from the department or division heads at the leadership meetings. But they don't have first-hand knowledge about what is really going on in the heart of the business—at the granular level—where the people are.

The tricky thing about being out of touch is that if you *are* out of touch, you don't know it. You think morale is good when it's not. You think the rollout of the new dealer communication system is going well when it's not. You think that your customers are happy when they're not.

A few years ago I was working with the leadership

team of an airline. The company had contracted for a comprehensive customer attitude and satisfaction survey, and at this meeting the results were to be revealed. As background, know that these executives were quite proud of delivering what they thought was the best customer experience in the business For them, customers came first. That's what they all said, that's what their slogans said, and that's what they believed was true.

It was at that meeting that I heard one of the most memorable lines from any executive, ever. He said, "The most important finding of the customer attitude and satisfaction study is this: our best customers hate our guts."

This airline was pretty much the only choice for fliers out of a handful of major cities. Thus, fliers had no choice. They flew the airline frequently, but hated everything about the service. The leadership team was clueless. They were guilty of believing their own advertising, which talked a great game about customer experience but didn't deliver.

How could these leaders be so oblivious to reality? Because they only talked to each other. They lived in an "aren't we great!" echo chamber. It was a case of business malpractice, created by leadership arrogance that made them believe only what they wanted to believe and listen to only the people who reinforced their wildly inaccurate judgements about their own performance.

In another instance of not knowing what was going on, I was in the back of a meeting room when the CEO onstage congratulated the group on the fabulously successful rollout of the new distribution system. "Give yourselves a hand!" The rollout had been fraught with problems and bugs, and everyone in the room knew it except the CEO. A guy sitting beside me put his head in his hands and said, "He doesn't have a clue."

Effective leaders know what's going on, and one of the ways they stay in touch with reality is that they spend time working in the business. Yes, I said *in* the business.

You read it in every leadership book and hear from every business motivational speaker: "Don't work *in* the business. Work *on* the business." Which means that you shouldn't be doing the work. You should be thinking and planning and strategizing.

OK. Fine. I get it. We all get it. Of course you have to do high-level thinking. But don't sit and think too much. The most effective business leaders I know are keenly aware of the nuts and bolts of the business. They know how their business works and whether or not it, in fact, *is* working. The worst leaders I've seen consider themselves to be above the fray, and those are the ones who are most at risk of not knowing what's really going on.

A group of friends and I recently stayed at a hotel whose slogan, which we saw everywhere in the hotel, is "We have a culture of Yes!" But the reality is that, no, they don't. They have a *slogan* of "Yes!" They have a culture of "we make you wait until you think your watch is broken." Without going into a list of the times we had to wait . . . and wait . . . and wait in the hotel lobby, at the front desk, and especially in the bar and restaurant, suffice it to say that their stated "culture of Yes!" was non-existent. Their reality was a culture of inattention bordering on incompetence. Leadership in that hotel either doesn't know what's going on or doesn't care.

One lesson for us all in that sad story is to know the difference between a slogan and reality. Just because you say you have a "culture of yes," or that you "exceed your customers' expectations," or that you're "better than the competition," doesn't mean it's true. As a leader, a big part of your job is to make sure that what you say your brand or your culture is all about matches up with reality. To do that you have to know what's happening in the trenches and on the front lines.

You'd definitely better know what your customers are saying about you: not necessarily what they're saying to your face, but what they're saying to others behind your back. Customers define your brand when they tell people what it's like to do business with you. Any leader worth his or her paycheck knows what their brand reality is on review sites and on social media.

Internally, go do some leadership by walking around (shout out to *The One Minute Manager* author Ken Blanchard) and actually talk with your people about what's happening every day at ground level. Get your hands dirty. Keep your ears open. Make sure that you are getting a continuous reality check.

There are tremendous payoffs in all sorts of ways for creating honest, open communication and feedback with employees, colleagues, vendor partners, customers, the community—everybody. It doesn't happen overnight. It takes time to create because it has to be built on a foundation of trust. Put in the time. Knowing what's really going on is essential not only to success, but to your very survival as a business.

Asking The Tough Questions

- *I know what's really going on. Yes/No*

- *If "yes"—I'm confident I know what's really going on because _____.*

- *Whether "yes" or "no," how will I ensure that I will always know what's going on within the organization?*

- *How will I/we know what's really going on with customers?*

- *What will we do to get our customers to give us ideas on how we can be better?*

- *What will we do to be sure that we are getting honest feedback from our employees?*

LEADERS TAKE ACTION, LEADERS RESPOND QUICKLY

There's a popular business saying that "all planning is good." Let's put that into perspective, because there's a new business reality that "slow is the new broken." If too much planning makes you slow, you're broken.

Why do so many leaders get stuck in what becomes endless planning for that new product, service, strategy, expansion, or initiative? Potentially great ideas die a slow death in planning hell because the leader wants to eliminate risk or make it foolproof. And sometimes there may also be an element of protecting his or her own skin involved. Ineffective leaders can sometimes live by the mantra of "Just Don't Mess Up!" and that doing nothing is the safest course.

Contrast that with one of my longtime clients, a very successful bank whose CEO has been an effective leader for decades. His mindset has changed as the realities of business have changed. Recently, in an interview with a business publication, he said, "We hit our goals about half the time. I have people ask if I'm OK with that. Well, you have to wonder how big, hairy, and audacious goals really are if you hit them 100% of the time." A lot of successful business leaders in the past wouldn't have tolerated a success rate of only 50%. Today's successful leader knows that you must risk to succeed.

My colleague in The Disruption Lab, Steve Little, says, "Moving beyond planning to experimentation and execution is essential for every organization. It is through experimentation and execution that real learning takes place, and it is real learning that fuels innovation." You have to not only lead through chaos but sometimes even create the chaos, because it's how you stay stable. To achieve stability by creating chaos sounds counterintuitive, but today it's absolutely true. And you must innovate to achieve stability in the market.

Today's successful leader will lead a team that is good at having ideas and equally good at killing them. Have a lot of ideas, take action quickly, and kill the bad ones quickly. Take what's left and go to market. You ship it, find out what's wrong with it, adjust, then press on. Quick to succeed. Quick to fail.

Helmuth von Moltke was the chief of staff of the Prussian army before World War I. Moltke had learned the strategies of war when battles consisted of men lining up in neat rows across from each other and exchanging musket fire. You could draw up your battle plan and stick with it, as most of the critical factors in the battle were predictable and would remain constant.

But in the 1880s, technology changed everything. Machine guns, heavy artillery, trains that could move troops more quickly than ever before all combined in a fluid, unpredictable dynamic that changed forever the planning of battle strategies. Moltke summed up this new reality when he said, "No battle plan survives first contact with the enemy." If you'd prefer a modern-era quote expressing the same reality, we need look no further than former heavyweight world champion boxer Mike Tyson, who said, "Everybody has a plan until they get punched in the mouth."

I'm not saying "don't plan." Of course you have to plan. Planning gives you direction, guides the organization and use of your resources, and informs your team. But then you roll out the plan and, inevitably, you get punched in the mouth. Just when you think you understand the situation, you blink and the situation has changed. Change has always been around, but it's never come as quickly or with as much impact as it does today. Thus, we need a different leadership mindset.

Change may take the form of a competitor who quickly copies what was your new, game-changing strategy; potential customers who say, "Nice try, but no thanks"; new technology that makes your offering obsolete; or an unexpected change in the economy (check your history books about 2008) that blows all great plans asunder.

When something like this happens to your company, leadership is a matter of how you respond. Like it or not, with all of our careful planning and precise strategizing, at some point the marketplace will punch you in the mouth, and it's then that you step up and become a leader. Yes, as a leader you plan. But the real leadership starts when reality blows the plan to pieces.

My wife, Annette, and I were having dinner with Julie and Charles May, whose company *bytes of knowledge* is a case study in my book, *Be the Best at What Matters Most*. We were talking about business, disruption, innovation, and great new ideas when Julie said, "Nothing is the right answer for very long."

Make it a mantra, because Julie absolutely nailed a fundamental truth about business today: "Nothing is the right answer for very long."

Give up the notion of waiting until you know your plan is perfect with no chance of failure before you act. You'll never get it perfect. Market realities (not to mention technology, people, competition, economies, etc.) will always be changing, and so your product, service, value propositions, strategies, and plans of all sorts must change, too, if you are to survive, much less thrive.

In 1978, Henry Mintzberg introduced the idea of emergent strategy. The idea is that the only strategy that makes sense in world of constant change is to react to a never-ending variety of unanticipated events. This drives a lot of business pundits over the edge. "But you can't be *reactive*! The horror! You have to be *proactive*, set a strategy in stone, and stick to it with absolute devotion!"

On what planet will that work? Because on Earth, that's simply not realistic. Yes, you have a strategy. But you have to know that you will, you *must* adjust that strategy to react to the stream of unpredictable changes in the marketplace that will inevitably take place. The key is that you react with clarity, purpose, and intention.

Through my work with The Disruption Lab, I've studied Alexander Osterwalder, who invented the Business Model Canvas, was a cofounder of strategyzer.com and coauthored *Business Model Generation,* which sold a million copies in 30 languages. In describing the leadership qualities necessary to succeed in an environment of continuous innovation, Osterwalder says, "In innovation one needs the ability to shape ideas, see patterns (in the market), deal with ambiguity, and rapidly test, throw away, and adapt ideas."

I think that's the key: "test, throw away, and adapt." Remember that we're not talking about values here. We're talking about tactics, strategies, and sometimes even your purpose. Your values should act as the stabilizing force that helps get you through the chaos of new ideas and change which are always followed by more new ideas and more change. But strategies and tactics are always temporary.

The bottom line is that effective leaders have a propensity to action, and they create organizations with that same mindset. Two friends of mine, both astute business thinkers and leaders, have valuable thoughts about action. Arnie Malham says, "If it's worth doing, it's worth doing wrong." (Buy his book, *Worth Doing Wrong: The Quest to Build a Culture That Rocks*.) The idea is that if your intention is to wait until it's perfect, with no chance to fail, then you most likely will never do it, and it's an opportunity lost. "Do it," Arnie says, "do it wrong. Then do it better." In much the same vein, consultant and business advisor Elizabeth Crook advises businesses to always ask, "What is the risk of *not* doing it?" We get so hung up on the potential dangers of doing something that we ignore what may be the much greater risk of doing nothing.

Whenever I work with a successful group of experienced leaders I ask, "How many of you have had ideas that you planned, implemented, and that ultimately didn't work?" Every hand in the room goes up. I then ask, "How many of you know that you will have and try more ideas that won't work?" If they're effective, successful leaders, every hand in the room goes up again. Leaders who struggle are much more likely to say that they've learned their lessons and from now on they will only have ideas that work. Baloney.

A successful leader knows when to say "go." A successful leader enters the fray and gets out in the middle of the competitive battlefield. You can sit in a conference room or a coffee shop, thinking and brainstorming and planning with your colleagues for days, months, or years. But sooner or later (and sooner is usually better) you need to put the idea into play and let the market give you feedback.

Asking The Tough Questions

- *I don't get stuck in planning. I take action quickly and decisively, knowing that I will adjust when necessary. Yes/No*

- *Are we going to try things that will not work out as we wanted them to? Yes*
  (I'm not giving you a "No" option. The answer is yes.)

- *When things don't work, do I respond constructively and in a way that moves us forward? Yes/No*

- *I kill ideas that don't work and won't work. Yes/No*

- *What are three things that I know I/we should take action on immediately?*

- *What will I do today to make that happen?*

- *What should we try/test to move us forward?*

- *What are the obstacles that keep me/us from taking action?*

- *What will I do today to begin to remove or overcome those obstacles?*

LEADERSHIP
AND DISRUPTION

Disruption. Go to any blog, article, or book about business today and you will likely be reading about disruption. The concept of innovative disruption came to the attention of many people through the book *The Innovator's Dilemma* by Clayton Christensen. Now everybody talks about disruption all the time, and there seem to be as many definitions for it as there are people using the word.

Christensen's definition is that disruptive innovation describes a process by which a product or service initially takes root in simple applications at the bottom of a market, typically by being less expensive and more accessible, and then relentlessly moves upmarket, eventually displacing established competitors. Another commonly used definition says that a disruptive innovation is an innovation that creates a new market and value network and eventually disrupts an existing market and value network, displacing established market-leading firms, products, and alliances.

I frequently come across the phrase "the threat of disruption." To me that's like saying "the threat of innovation." Both disruption and innovation are threats only if you're not the one doing it.

For leaders of a successful business today, one thing is clear. You will most likely face the challenge of having to sustain and grow the success of your existing business while, at the same time, disrupting that business with what will come next. In effect, you may very well end up being the architect of the strategy that puts you out of business, which is a very good thing. The alternative is that somebody else puts you out of business.

It's a leadership challenge of the highest order, because it goes against the thinking that current success can easily create. Success makes us want to keep doing what we're doing, and, if we're smart, do it better. That's a worthy pursuit, and of course you want to sustain and grow your current success as well as you can for as long as you can. The problem with current success is that it can lead to complacency and can blind you to what you may need to do going forward to not only succeed, but survive.

I've mentioned that I'm associated with The Disruption Lab, a consulting group that helps companies create and implement disruptive innovation strategies. My colleagues, Phil Gibbs, Katie Sulkowski, Steve Little, and I are in a continuous learning loop about disruption. One thing that we've learned is that it is very difficult to disrupt from within. You can innovate and improve internally, and indeed you have to if you are to sustain and grow your business. But to move on to that next thing that you must be to thrive in the future, to really make the leap to a new reality, you have to disrupt.

It's hard because it goes against a natural inclination to protect and pour all of your resources into what's working now. Leaders today understand the need to devote a portion of your resources in terms of time, money, and people to pursuing the next thing, which is, in effect, a startup business. And like all startups, it might not work.

This startup project happens while you are sustaining and growing your present business success. It's a tremendous challenge and quite the mindset juggling act. Creating a startup is a learning process. For a company used to success, starting a new business which will go through setbacks and sometimes outright defeat is a daunting prospect, to say the least.

What you should seriously consider is taking the disruption effort outside the company. Set up your disruption team or person, as a separate entity and say "Do to us what Netflix did to Blockbuster. Go forth and disrupt." Get them the support that they need from an outside resource, and turn them loose.

I spoke with Steve Little of The Disruption Lab about disruptive innovation and what it means to an organization.

Joe: *Steve, what does the term "disruptive innovation" really mean?*

Steve: Disruptive innovation is about creating new markets or displacing incumbents in existing markets. In the strict definition proffered by Clay Christensen, disruptive innovation creates a simpler, more accessible, less expensive product or service that opens an untapped market, generally down-market. Today disruptive innovation is often accomplished by employing new business models and leveraging proven digital technologies.

Joe: *What I've discovered is that true disruptive innovation is not only hard, but it may actually be in conflict with strategies that are currently working for a company.*

Steve: The cultural characteristics underpinning successful disruptive innovations are somewhat unique and not necessarily ones that you want to foster throughout your entire organization. When considering efficiency and sustaining innovations, alignment with corporate strategy is imperative. With disruptive innovation, however, attempts to align with corporate strategy may, in fact, hamper innovation efforts.

Joe: *What would be an example of a characteristic that a leader and a company has to have to create disruptive innovation?*

Steve: One would be high risk tolerance. Contrary to the sentiment in the movie *Apollo 13*, failure *is* an option; in fact, it's an expectation.

Joe: *But failure isn't something that we naturally seek out if we're trying to run a successful business.*

Steve: In your core business, how much failure can you afford? Those responsible for operating your business need to have a mindset closer to that expressed in *Apollo 13*, "failure is not an option." You need to perform and deliver as flawlessly as possible every time. So there is a cadre in your core business that you do not want operating with a high risk tolerance.

Joe: *So you're suggesting that there should be people in your business with a very different mindset.*

Steve: Yes. One not constrained by "how this might impact our core business."

Disruptive innovators must be free to explore solutions that may cannibalize or completely displace your core business. The focus is finding a better way to satisfy the "job to be done." This may mean completely obsoleting significant company assets and long-term commitments. For those in your core business, there must be a sensitivity to maximizing the return on corporate assets. Throwing out current assets and starting all over is not an option you want your core operators focused on.

Joe: *So you're suggesting a whole different set of rules or standards for those who are the disruptors.*

Steve: Applying typical success metrics to disruptive innovation is misguided at best and more likely fatal to disruptive innovation initiatives. While ROI may be an excellent measure for prioritizing efficiency and sustaining innovations, it is nonsensical when applied to disruptive innovations. Do I want my core business to be concerned about ROI? You bet! Should that be a focus of my innovation team? Absolutely not, at least not in the beginning. The innovation team needs success metrics related to learning and validating hypotheses. Fundamentally, the metrics that drive the behavior of operators are necessarily different than the metrics driving the behavior of disruptive innovators.

Joe: *How do you create an environment supportive of disruptive innovation?*

Steve: Disruptive innovators need to operate in open, collaborative environments. Working with customers, suppliers, outside business and technical resources, trade associations, and perhaps even competitors are often necessary for disruptive innovators. Open environments strain the typical view of protecting intellectual property and potential strategies. While this may be OK for my disruptive innovation teams, I generally do not want my core operating teams functioning with a cavalier attitude about intellectual property and core strategies.

Joe: *It sounds like the disruptors have to be separated from the core operators of the business.*

Steve: The culture of disruptive innovators and core operators are necessarily different. For this reason, it is often beneficial to have an "innovation veil" of separation. An organization creates an innovation veil in various ways. Decades ago, skunk works became a popular approach. Today we see corporate innovation labs, incubators, and accelerators, all of which attempt to provide some separation from the core business.

Joe: *Thank you, Steve.*

One key point is that when you think and talk about disruptive innovation, you should separate that concept from sustaining innovation. Look at sustaining innovation as the process of adding value to your current business. But adding value to what you already do isn't disruption. Think of disruption as the process of discovering and developing the new business that you should go into. The *next* business.

You can't claim to be an effective leader today if you are not thinking about what disruption means for your business. We can develop a false sense of security if our businesses are doing well and our best customers love us. But more and more often we find that "We're doing great!" turn out to be famous last words. Do that thought exercise with your team of asking the question, "What might put us out of business in the next three years?" See where it takes you. It just might take you to your next big opportunity.

A leader today has to be willing to do more than tweak and improve what already exists. She's got to be willing to possibly blow things up for the sake of getting to the *next* thing.

Asking The Tough Questions

- *I have thought about what disruption (the Christensen definition) might mean for our company both as a threat and an opportunity. Yes/No*

- *What are ten potential disruptors of our business?*

- *What should we begin to do to replace our current business with what should come next?*

- *Should we pursue disruption (the Christensen definition) as part of our strategy?*

- *Who should participate in our decisions about disruption?*

LEADERS
CREATE VALUE

Jony Ive, chief design officer for Apple, said, "It's very easy to be different, but very difficult to be better." Any questions? I believe that Ive has absolutely hit on a core competitive reality, one that leaders should understand clearly. The goal isn't to be different. The goal is to be better.

I cringe a little when I hear a leader setting up "let's be different" as the goal for the organization. If everyone wears a funny hat, you're different. Effective leaders are focused on better, not different. Of course, if you are better, then by definition you'll be different, but it in ways that matter and create value.

Imagine a baseball player asking, "How can I swing the bat in a way that's different from any other baseball player?" Really? Who cares? What's the point?

For the baseball player, the right question is, "How can I get more hits?"

Many businesses ask themselves "How can we be different?" Again . . . who cares? For a business, the right question is, "How can we add value?" Adding value will, by definition, involve doing something differently, and innovating, and maybe even disrupting. The point is to be focused on the right thing, which is creating value. A focus on being different can be an exercise in pure distraction.

Here's the problem: if you start off by saying "Let's be different!" then you can easily go down the path of creating nothing but gimmicks. But if you are focused on adding value, on being better than your competition, you will quite naturally end up innovating or disrupting to some degree, and you will be different, but in a way that has true worth. And, if you provide greater value, then you are different in the only way that matters to the marketplace.

The leadership mindset is always focused on creating value.

Asking The Tough Questions

- *We are better than our competition. Yes/No*

- *I know that for a fact because*

  _____.

- *Looking at every facet of our business, where do we need to be better?*

- *(This is obviously a huge question that will require a lot of time and thought to answer. You will then have to continually answer it again and again—forever.)*

- *What are the first steps I will take today to make us better?*

- *In what specific areas?*

- *How will I know we're making progress?*

- *How will I bring my team into the effort to achieve continuous improvement?*

LEADING A CUSTOMER-FOCUSED TEAM

Today's successful leader is customer-focused and leads a customer-focused team. That, as Tom Peters would say, is a blinding flash of the obvious. No leader can be successful in today's marketplace unless she and her team understand that, ultimately, the organization exists to create and keep customers.

That's certainly not a new idea. But here's what is new: how the behavior of existing customers is the single most important factor in your ability to win and keep new customers. More specifically, it's what your existing customers say about you to potential customers that determines your success or failure. We do business today in a word-of-mouth-driven marketplace. Today's leader has to understand what that means in terms of focus and what matters most to the entire team.

I was recently co-leader of a program that took leaders from a range of businesses to New York and Barcelona to study innovative companies. In Barcelona, we had lunch at Disfrutar, named 18th best restaurant in the world on The World's Best Restaurants list. Follow the trail from customer experience to creating new customers and see how the leadership mindset there drives it all.

The food at Disfrutar is truly amazing. Our 20+ course luncheon left us without words sufficient to describe the experience. *Condé Nast Traveler*'s recent review of the restaurant said, "A tasting menu at Disfrutar is like a performance: There is fire, ice, smoke, and lots of flavor and color. This is why Disfrutar can only really be experienced in the tasting menu format. Casañas, Castro, and Xatruch's creations are playful and unpredictable, often surprising us by telling our eyes one thing but sending our taste buds a completely different message."

The food is at the center of the Disfrutar experience. It is different in the only way that counts, in that it is better. There's lots going on in terms of innovation with their food, but the bottom line is that it's so good that really defies description.

Of course, the other component in the customer experience is the staff and how they treat customers.

The *Condé Nast Traveler* review says, "Disfrutar may be serious about its food, but that doesn't mean it hires snooty waiters. On the contrary, servers at Disfrutar are warm, laid-back, and eager to help."

Here's an example of the kind of customer focus that you experience from everyone that works at Disfrutar.

At the end of our meal, our server took orders for coffee or after-luncheon drinks. Paul Rosser, a successful entrepreneur from England and part of our innovation study group, ordered an espresso. When the server brought everyone's orders back a few moments later, Paul had left the table. The server said, "I don't want this to cool off while he's gone. I'll make him a fresh one when he returns."

Now, follow the trail from us as customers to what we told people after the trip. We all told lots of people in face-to-face conversations about how wonderful Disfratur is. We all were, and still are, saying things like, "If you are ever in Barcelona, make reservations to go to Disfrutar. It's the restaurant experience of a lifetime." But the real impact is what we all have done on social media. On Facebook, Linkedin, Instagram, Snapchat, Twitter, and other platforms, we have told countless people that they should do business with Disfrutar.

Making sure that the espresso was fresh and hot was a seemingly small gesture. It was a small and simple example of getting it right. But the potential positive impact of that customer experience, combined with countless other similar experiences being created by the entire staff all day and night, is huge. That evening after our luncheon experience, as we were talking about Disfrutar and what makes it so great, those of us who had been sitting with Paul all remarked on the kind of leadership that imbues a culture with the desire to get everything right, for every customer, every single time.

Replacing Paul's espresso with a fresh one was the result of the leadership mindset of the owner/chefs and the culture they had created. It's also a lesson in the payoff that comes with relentless training and reinforcement of what's expected. Showing that you care about small things done with extraordinary attention can be achieved by any organization, but it doesn't happen because of a memo, signs in the break room, or the occasional mention at employee meetings. It happens when leadership thinks about it, talks about it, and models it all day long, every day. It becomes part of the organizational DNA.

A key element in my leadership workshop, "Leading the Customer-Focused Team," is that effective leaders must understand what drives the buying decisions of today's customers. While advertising and traditional marketing certainly still have their place in the effort to gain customers, there's been a monumental shift in the marketplace. The impact of what you say about yourself through any media or on any platform pales in comparison to the impact of what your customers say about you. We are in an age of a new customer moment of truth. That moment is when any potential customer for any product or service goes on the internet to see what others are saying. If there are ratings, i.e., 1 to 5 stars, and a business has an average rating of 1.5 stars, it's game over. The potential customer moves on to another potential choice. If, however, that business has an average rating of 4.5 stars, then there is a great likelihood that this will be the new customer's choice.

Impact on the customer experience has to be considered with any and every decision that you make. Certainly, when today's leader thinks about what matters most for the organization, customer experience and its impact on creating positive word of mouth has to be given top priority.

Asking The Tough Questions

- *As the leader, I keep the team focused on the customer experience. Yes/No*

- *Everyone on our team is dedicated to enabling our organization to deliver exceptional customer experiences. Yes/No*

- *We continually train our people, and we are relentless in driving a culture of exceptional customer experience. Yes/No*

- *We are intentional about creating positive word of mouth by existing customers to bring new customers to us. Yes/No*

- *What will I do immediately to ensure that we are customer-focused?*

- *What will I do immediately to ensure that we are consistently delivering an exceptional customer experience to every customer, every time?*

- *What will we do to find out what our customer experience really is from the customer's point of view?*

- *How will we measure performance so that we know exactly what level of customer experience we are delivering?*

- *Who in the organization is ultimately responsible for the customer experience we deliver?*

- *How will we encourage positive customer word of mouth?*

LEADERS REPEAT AND REINFORCE

There is a particular mindset and behavior that I've observed in almost every successful leader I've ever worked with. The idea is this: they talk about what's important, and they talk about it all the time. They repeat and reinforce the mission, values, culture, vision, purpose—whatever is important. They repeat and reinforce it every day without end.

I'm not talking about scripts or memorizing. I'm not talking about everybody being able to recite something that you've got on a poster. I'm talking about making the most important ideas part of your organizational DNA, so that it's impossible to work there without everyone knowing in their minds and hearts what matters most. When you achieve that, you create an enormous competitive advantage. But you have to embrace the fact that, as the leader, it's your responsibility. It is your job to make that happen.

Jonathan Tisch, CEO of Loews Hotels, said, "The decisions I make about Loews are meaningless unless I get buy-in from my 7,500 co-workers." How do you get buy-in? The single most effective way is to repeat and reinforce.

In my experience, no one understood and lived that concept better than Joe Scarlett when he was chairman of the board and CEO of the mega-successful national retailer, Tractor Supply Company. I interviewed Joe for my book *Becoming a Category of One*. I'm going to share part of that interview with you here, because Joe absolutely nails the power of "repeat and reinforce."

Joe Calloway: *What differentiates Tractor Supply Company from the competition?*

Joe Scarlett: One strong differentiating point is our culture. We've carved out this mission and values statement that we really live and really practice. When you compare us to other similar employers, they tend very often to have a very loose and undefined culture. In our company you can talk to almost anybody and they'll be able to recite back our mission, because it's there and they hear it all the time.

JC: *You talk about "living the mission statement." How do you pull that off? What's the secret to making a mission statement "real" instead of just something that you read at the company meetings once a year?*

JS: Twice a year we have our big company-wide meetings. And at every one of those meetings over the years, they hear from me talking about "work hard, have fun, make money, take care of the customer," and so on. And I talk about it non-stop. Whenever they see me coming, they know I'm going to talk about it.

For years, at an elevating pace, more of our people are doing the same thing. We just finished our summer meetings. I show up on the last day to talk about the mission, and unbeknownst to me, on the first day of the meeting, the district managers have already done the same thing. More and more people are taking ownership of it. It's in our publication. The column I write for the company magazine is always tied in one way or another to our mission. I can't tell you how, other than we talk about it all the time. And everybody's really taking a sense of ownership. They've heard it for so long and so repetitively that everyone buys into it and it becomes a way of life.

Every quarter we have a meeting here at the store support center. We introduce everyone who's new to the company at the beginning of that meeting. At the end of the meeting I tell all those new people to stick around and for a half an hour with every new employee talking about our mission and our values, and I welcome them to the company that way.

In our stores when someone starts working for us there's an introductory video with me and Jim Wright, our president, talking about the mission and the values. It's just everywhere. I don't think there's any real secret to it other than just being repetitive. Some companies just plaster their mission up on the walls and let it sit there. We keep talking about it all the time. It's got a life of its own.

JC: *Is talking about mission and values all the time the key to leadership?*

JS: Yes. I guess you could put it that way. We are consistent about what we're doing. We say the same thing over and over again, and we focus on the same issues. I think there's a sense of leadership because we're consistently talking about working hard, having fun, making money, taking care of the customer.

We talk about the same thing over and over again so we're always going in the same direction.

It's interesting that when we hire people from other companies, a couple of the things that they always say is that they like our business and our niche and our customers. But they also like the fact that we don't change direction every day. So many companies are going one way one month and another way the next month, and they are always chasing the latest fad. We don't go for the latest fad. We stay consistently doing the same thing over and over again. They love that. They also like the fact that we've got a strong set of values and there's never any compromising. Ethics is ethics, and you either do it the right way or you go somewhere else. In other companies sometimes they might see some bending of the rules, and they get confused by that.

Every year we have a discussion here about what the theme of the manager's meeting should be. The people planning the meeting get excited and say, "Oh yeah, we've got to have a theme! Every meeting has to have a theme!" And I keep saying, "Okay, but whatever it is, let's not make too big a deal out of it, because the theme is really the same every year. We're going to talk about our mission and our values."

JC: *Thank you, Joe.*

I could give you pages of stories of effective leaders who would say basically the same thing that Joe said. Let me leave you with two final examples of the "repeat and reinforce" idea. Marty Grunder, president and CEO of Grunder Landscaping Company, is pretty much my go-to example of the mindset of today's successful leader. He recently said, "Our core values at Grunder Landscaping are constantly discussed and reinforced. We have learned that you must constantly talk about what matters most."

And finally, I will always remember this statement from Alwyn Lewis. I was doing a lot of leadership development work with YUM Brands, and Alwyn was a senior executive with the company. He once said, "If you ever see me in front of a group of employees and I'm not talking about customer service, call the FBI. Because aliens have taken over my body."

"Repeat and reinforce" is what every effective leader I've ever worked with does. It's not optional. It's how you build and guide a team that has clarity on what matters most, where they're going, and how to get there.

Asking The Tough Questions

- *As a leader, I do a great job of repeating and reinforcing what's most important to our organization. Yes/No*

- *What will I do to ensure that we do a better job of repeating and reinforcing?*

- *Whose support do I need in accomplishing this?*

- *When will I talk with them about it?*

GREAT LEADERS HAVE GREAT MEETINGS (AND DON'T GIVE SPEECHES)

I've been a part of thousands of corporate meetings and events. I've seen extraordinary meetings that made a significant positive difference and I've seen absolutely dreadful meetings that were a waste of everyone's time and sometimes even had a negative effect. Meetings have become such an omnipresent factor in business today that to be an effective leader, you have to know how to make meetings great. Every meeting is an opportunity to inform in a meaningful way and to create alignment, engagement, and commitment.

Let me start with what may seem to be an odd suggestion for leaders: Don't give speeches. Consider these two statements: "Our CEO gave a speech about the company's future." vs. "Our CEO talked with us about the company's future" There's a subtle but significant difference in those two statements. Over the years I've worked with a lot of leaders on how to give effective presentations. The key is mindset. They say to me, "Help me give better speeches." I say, "OK. the first thing is, don't ever give speeches."

One reason that so many speeches just aren't effective is that leaders "get in their heads" about how they think a speech is supposed to sound. If leaders would think in terms of "I'm going to tell them about this," instead of, "I'm going to give a speech about this," they'd almost always be more effective.

Peggy Noonan, *Wall Street Journal* columnist and former speechwriter for President Ronald Reagan, had some of the best advice I've ever heard for speakers. She said "Don't be slick. They've seen slick. Be you. They haven't seen that." Robert Herjavec, founder of Herjavec Group and a "shark" on the hit TV show, *Shark Tank*, said, "Just be yourself. You need to command your audience's attention, and you can't do that if you too busy trying to be something you're not."

I've seen business leaders whom I think are among the best speakers in the world. Some of them are light years better than a lot of "professional speakers." Not one of them is "speechy." They all talk with their audiences in a way that conveys, "Here's what I want to share with you. Let me tell you about it." As you prepare for whatever next presentation you've got coming up, don't prepare a speech. Get clear and grounded in what you want them to know and understand, and then talk with them about it. For most speakers, a simple key word or phrase outline will serve you extremely well.

One of the most effective ways to have a great meeting is to think of it as a conversation. In *Fast Company* magazine, veteran speaking expert Nancy Duarte predicts that presentations will become ever more interactive. "People are losing their patience with lectures," Duarte said. "Instead, they want to have conversations with speakers."

At a business convention in Saskatoon, Saskatchewan, I was one of four keynote speakers. Three of us got our audiences fully engaged as participants. The meeting planner told me afterward that their participant feedback is overwhelmingly in favor of wanting more interaction in the keynote sessions.

Don't get me wrong. There's definitely still a

place for the speaker who does all the talking and can inspire, motivate, and inform an audience with a fabulous one-way presentation. That's fine. But leaders today must consider that the days are coming to an end for meetings and conventions where people spend six or more hours a day sitting in straight rows in total silence, listening to lectures.

A live meeting is, in many ways, no different than a website. People want to engage and interact, whether it's online or in a meeting. We are shifting from having "attendees" to having "participants," and more meetings everyday are moving in that direction. Think of it this way: Can you imagine anyone planning a meeting today and saying, "We don't want our people actively engaged or participating. We want them to just sit there, be quiet, and listen to speeches all day." Really?

Years ago I quit giving traditional speeches in favor of having conversations in more interactive formats and workshops. I may be the one in the front of the room, but the last thing I want to do is give a one-way lecture with mind-numbing PowerPoint. What I'll do is talk *with* you about leadership. It will feel like and be a conversation.

I recently led a leadership workshop in Chicago with a $100 million sales company. I was in the slot right after the CEO's opening remarks. In his very conversational, very effective presentation, the CEO said "We've designed this critically important meeting to encourage maximum engagement and interaction during all presentations. This meeting has to create real value." He's a leader after my own heart. It's hard to go wrong when your goal is to create value.

I love what Jeff Bezos does with some of the leadership meetings at Amazon. The meeting starts with everyone quietly reading something considered relevant or potentially meaningful for the organization. They're all reading the same thing. After they finish reading, they open the floor to a discussion of what they've read. The ideas flow, different points of view are heard, and value is created.

This kind of meeting matches up with an observation that came out of Northstar Travel Group's Independent Planner Education Conference/2017:

> Sessions need to move from monologue to dialog to polylogue, where participants are talking together in a group. Speakers, then, become facilitators of learning. That's not a comfortable skill for a lot of speakers. For them, this is a growing-edge skill . . . it is the skill of the future.

It's a leadership skill of the present.

One extremely effective format to consider, which I've used many times with great success, is on-stage interviews or conversations. Sometimes the original agenda has called for the CEO to speak for an hour and then for me do my session for an hour. I'll have them change the agenda to cut both the CEO and me back to thirty minutes each. After that he or she and I sit down on stage for a one-hour conversation about the important topics and issues.

A home construction company in Dallas was experiencing great success but was about to undergo some really serious changes. The employees were questioning why they needed to change when things were going so well. The CEO and I talked about it on stage in a very conversational interview. It wasn't scripted. It was real. Afterwards the employees felt that they now understood the rationale for the changes and they also got a sense of how excited and enthusiastic the CEO was about the changes. The conversation conveyed it much more effectively than any speech he could have given.

Here's another tip for effective meetings. When planning what will be a relatively long meeting or event, never let your goal be to fill time slots. If a meeting planning committee starts with, "OK, we've got five time slots to fill on day one of the meeting, so let's get started," I know it's probably going to be a bad meeting. "Filling time slots" isn't the way to get the most out of an event.

When I work with leaders who are planning an event, the first thing I have them do is reach consensus and get clarity on exactly what they they are wanting to accomplish, both short- and long-term. What immediate effect do you want to create? What's the long-term effect you're after? How will this event advance your strategy? What's the point?

Beware of this trap: "We need a sixty-minute presentation." Why? Is it because your "keynote" speeches have always been sixty minutes? Is sixty minutes the amount of time that will maximize the positive impact and value of the presentation? How do you know? Or are you saying that it's sixty minutes because that's the way you've always done it? That's called being stuck.

It all goes back to what you're trying to accomplish. You may find it most productive to have a session go for five hours instead of one. Instead of your annual meeting being three days, maybe it should be two, or one, or five! What's the point of the meeting? How can you best advance your strategy?

Here's a final tip that can make all the difference

in your meeting: do the unexpected. Be human. Be real. The normal, expected thing to do at a meeting is to have the executives and leaders of a company give presentations to the employees. One of the most powerful and effective things I've ever experienced in a meeting reversed that formula.

My client was one of the most respected insurance companies in the country.

In the planning for their annual retreat for the top one hundred leaders in the company, they decided that one of their two main goals was to create a renewed sense of commitment to the purpose of the company and their commitment to customers.

I suggested something that they'd never done before, and the CEO gave me permission to do it.

I opened the final session of the two-day event with a conversation about what really constituted the brand of the company. My premise, with which the leaders agreed, was that the brand was created one customer experience at a time, and that the people who were most directly responsible for that wasn't them, the top one hundred leaders, but the front line employees with direct customer contact.

To the surprise of the leaders, I then brought onto the stage five customer service representatives from one of the company's call centers. They each took a seat on a tall barstool and we began to talk about their jobs and why what they did was important to them. As the CSRs told their stories and talked what it meant to them to work for a company that took such good care of customers, you could have heard a pin drop in the room.

At the end of the conversation, those top one hundred executive leaders gave a loud, heartfelt, and tearful standing ovation to the CSRs. The CEO took the stage, personally thanked each employee, and then told the group that it was the most meaningful and powerful thing he'd ever experienced in a business meeting.

Remember that a meeting, whether it's your leadership team, a customer forum, or the regular Monday morning meeting with twelve employees from a particular department, is one of your greatest opportunities to teach, inform, and inspire. Great leaders are intentional. Be fully intentional about every meeting.

Asking The Tough Questions

- *I am completely prepared and know exactly what I want to convey and accomplish when I give a presentation. Yes/No*

- *Are we stuck in the rut of planning and conducting our meetings in a certain way, simply because we've always done it that way? Yes/No*

- *At our next meeting, and for all future meetings, what immediate effect do we want to create?*

- *What's the long-term effect we want to create?*

- *How will this event or meeting advance our strategy?*

- *What's the point of the meeting?*

- *How can we best plan our meetings with clarity and intention?*

LEADING AN INNOVATIVE TEAM

Do you have to continually improve? Do you have to always be adding value? Do you need a steady flow of new ideas in order to stay competitive? Do you need your team to be innovative? Of course the answer to all of those questions is an unequivocal "yes." So how do effective leaders make that a reality?

Here's how many of them try. They get everyone together for an "innovation retreat." They have creative consultants come in and put everyone through games and exercises designed to foster creative thinking. At some point the team splits into smaller groups and there's a competition to build, for example, a boat that will actually float while carrying a loaf of bread. They have to build it out of a pile of completely disparate, unrelated things and parts that make no sense at all.

But, just like the crew of Apollo 13, they put their

mish-mash of parts together into some semblance of something that functions, at least to a degree, as it is designed to function. The loaf of bread successfully rests on the top of the boat, at least for a while, and then they all vote on who made the best boat. Yaaaaay! Now we've got an innovative team at work! Mission accomplished!

Except you know better. It really doesn't work that way. Don't get me wrong, those creativity sessions can be fun and useful to a degree. But it's rare, if ever, that they result in lasting innovation for the organization. So what does work?

This is what works, and it's what the most innovative companies in the world do each and every day: you look for good ideas *out there*, bring them back and adapt them to your own use *here*. Boom. That's it.

It's called adaptive innovation. It's what a car manufacturer was doing when it sent engineers to study a five-star hotel for ideas on customer experience. It's what an award-winning hospital was doing when they took a team to Japan to study the manufacturing processes of a leading car manufacturer for ideas on efficiency and effectiveness. It's what Susan from the dental clinic is doing when she comes to work one day with an idea for improving patient care that she got when she was getting her car serviced over the weekend.

Wait a minute. Improving dental patient care from something that a car service shop is doing? Yes. Exactly. That's the way it works. When I was the co-leader of a group of executives and business owners on a trip to Barcelona, Spain, one of our main purposes was to get ideas from the thirty companies that we visited. It wasn't so that we could copy the ideas, but so that we could adapt them to different arenas and markets. Adaptive innovation.

The great advantage of this approach to innovation is that you, your leadership team, and your employees don't have to be creative geniuses to make it work. You all just have to keep your eyes open and pay attention to what you see that's working out there. You hold yourselves accountable by creating a simple, quick process through which people report in and then you assign responsibility for taking the best ideas and running with them.

There is great truth in the old cliché, "It's *not* rocket science!"

I'm a fan of the Disney Institute. It's a look behind the scenes at how Disney is intentional about every little thing that happens in the parks. If you go through the Disney Institute course and don't come back with a ton of new ideas for your organization, then check your pulse. But you don't have to go to Disney for ideas that you can adapt and use. You can go just about anywhere.

I was leading a leadership retreat in Hollywood, California, in a hotel that was connected to a shopping mall. I gave the group ninety minutes to split up and go through the mall on their own with one assignment: find at least three ideas you could take back to your company and put to work. No one came back with less than seven ideas. Some had as many as fifteen. They were buzzing like a bee hive with ideas for innovations and improvements that had been right in front of them the whole time, but that they simply hadn't been looking for.

As a leader, your job is to make innovation part of everyone's job. There are simply no excuses for not using this adaptive innovation approach. It takes no special skill set, it's is available to every single person in your organization, and you can start doing it tomorrow.

Asking The Tough Questions

- *Our organization is continually innovating.*
  Yes/No

- *I know this is true because*
  _____.

- *What will I do to get our team to look for ideas that we can use?*

- *What will be our ongoing process to be sure that these ideas are heard?*

- *How will we proceed in making sure that we take action on these ideas?*

- *Who will be responsible for this?*

THE 3 THINGS

I saved the best for last. If not the best idea in the book, then it's certainly one of the most immediately applicable. One of the central ideas that I teach and that leaders find most helpful is that you can have 3 Things that guide your daily activities as a company, as a team or department, and as an individual.

The 3 Things are principles for action that, if you get them right every single day, will absolutely assure your success. No one can tell you what your 3 Things are, and in my leadership workshops, I don't tell you. You figure it out yourself. It's a little like the old movie *City Slickers*, in which Billy Crystal's character, Mitch, asks Jack Palance's character, Curly, what the meaning of life is. Curly says "One thing. Just one thing. You stick to that." Mitch asks what the one thing is. Curly replies, "That's what you have to find out."

My 3 Things idea isn't the meaning of life, but it's a great way to organize your thoughts and activities, and those of your team, around what matters most. It also serves to keep people focused on high-return activities.

These are arranged in what I think of as a kind of cascading relationship, meaning that the company has 3 Things, each team or department has the 3 Things that will contribute to the company, and each individual has 3 Things that will help drive the team's and the company's goals. You test and refine the ideas to be sure you've nailed exactly the right ones to insure your success and the success of the organization. You then take the 3 Things approach through the entire organization.

One of my favorite examples of the 3 Things concept is the way that one of my clients, a successful trucking company, uses it to drive consistently excellent performance through the entire organization. Imagine that you are the CEO of a trucking company. Here's how the 3 Things idea might work for you.

Rather than think that everyone in the company has 1,000 things to do everyday to make your purpose or vision become a reality, take the view that the company, each leader, each department, and each employee has three things that they should focus on every day. If they execute on those three things with excellence and consistency, the company and each person in it will succeed.

For your trucking company as a whole, I use my trucking company client as a wonderful example of how it works:

1. Pick it up when you said you would;

2. Deliver it when you said you would;

3. Deliver it intact and all there.

For that trucking company, that's it. If they do these three things better than their competition each and every day, they win. Each team within the company has their 3 Things, and so does each individual.

Consider your role as a leader and what your daily 3 Things should be. One CEO that I've worked with for years says that his 3 Things he has to get right every day are:

1. Protect the culture;

2. Listen;

3. Advance the strategy.

Your 3 Things might be totally different, but what this CEO's 3 Things do for him is help keep him focused on what he believes matters most in his role as leader and for the success of the company.

My 3 Things have remained constant for years. They are:

1. Improve the product;

2. Be easy and a pleasure to work with;

3. Respond immediately to clients, prospects, and partners.

I am easily distracted by new ideas. I absolutely love the next idea. That is a good quality for an entrepreneurial leader, but it can also pull you into the weeds. Knowing my 3 Things helps me differentiate between a distraction and a true opportunity.

For a successful fast food restaurant chain, their 3 Things are:

1. Serve only the freshest, highest-quality food;

2. With the highest-quality customer service;

3. In a spotless, sparkling clean environment.

With something like "the highest-quality customer service," you have to break that down into very specific standards that everyone understands. The 3 Things can't be slogans. They have to be guidelines that you take into the trenches with you every single day. Remember that the purpose is to keep the company, each team, and each individual focused on high-return activities.

Now here's where the smaller minds who have to complicate absolutely everything will say things like, "But it can't be that simple! It's not that easy!"

In fact, yes, it can be that simple, and that's the very thing you want to get to: simplicity. Of course we all have lots to do, but effective leaders are able to filter out the noise, stay focused, and keep the organization focused. And as for it not being easy, indeed it's not. Winning in business is never easy, which is why not everyone can do it. But it's much easier if you and your entire organization are focused each day on the 3 Things that matter most.

Let's review this one more time. Step one is to establish the 3 Things that the company must get right each day to win, and those will be based on and driven by your vision, mission, goals, or overall purpose statement. From there you take it to each division, department, or team. Each of those will have their 3 Things to focus on daily in order to help the company achieve its 3 Things. Each individual, including leaders, will then have their 3 Things to help their particular team achieve its goals.

I hear leaders talk of having a thousand things to do every day. Wow. I can't imagine it. Usually, it's leaders who are struggling that feel overwhelmed by all that's on their plate. Eli Manning once said, "Pressure is what you feel when you don't know what the hell you're doing." Leaders who are succeeding will say that there are a handful of things that determine their success or failure and that their job is to stay focused on those things and make sure that the rest of the company is, too. Putting it another way, they know what the hell they're doing.

Leaders who are struggling will forcefully make the case that theirs is a very complicated business, totally unlike any other, and that it's extremely difficult to make it all work the way that it should. The successful leader will tend to say, "You know, at the end of the day, this is a pretty simple business. If we get a few key things right and do them better than our competitors, we win. It's not easy. In fact, it's hard. But it's not all that complicated."

I get more positive feedback from clients on the effectiveness of the 3 Things idea than just about any other idea I know. It's not theory. It's being used day in and day out by companies and individuals to create focus and much greater productivity.

Identify your 3 Things. Execute with consistency and excellence.

This can change everything.

Asking The Tough Questions

- *What are the 3 Things that our company must do every day to assure success?*
- *What are the 3 Things each team or department must do to assure success?*
- *(This will likely be different for each team.)*
- *What are the 3 Things that I must do as a leader to assure success?*
- *How will I be sure that every team and individual has identified their 3 Things to do each day for success?*
- *What will I do to start this process in the organization?*

WHAT'S YOUR LEADERSHIP MINDSET?

I leave you with a couple of final thoughts.

There are so many things over which a leader has no control. But you have total control over your mindset. You can make a conscious, intentional choice about how you think and define your role and responsibilities as a leader.

The business news today has countless examples of companies in trouble as well as companies that are booming. The deciding factor at each end of that performance spectrum is leadership. You simply can't succeed long-term with weak leadership, and truly effective leaders can turn around companies that seemed like lost causes.

Mindset is mostly about attitude. It's about the way you approach and respond to the world around you. It's all a choice. It's a truism that you can't always choose what happens, but you can always choose your response to what happens.

You can choose your attitude. You can choose your mindset.

Choose wisely. Choose with intention.

Asking The Tough Questions

- *I choose my mindset. Yes.*

ABOUT THE AUTHOR

Joe Calloway is an author, speaker, and consultant on business leadership. He designs and delivers workshops and interactive keynote speeches for leadership meetings and retreats. He is the author of eight books on business performance and leadership.

Joe's workshop/keynote titles include:

The Leadership Mindset
How Today's Successful Business Leaders Think
Success today requires a new leadership mindset. Simplify, clarify, focus, innovate to create value, even disrupt . . . these are all parts of the mindset of today's successful leader. Participants will gain new perspectives on effective leadership, and will discover a simple, powerful process that creates a daily focus on high return activities for leaders and their teams.

Leading The Customer Focused Team
Winning And Keeping Customers In Today's
New Market Reality

Customer experience drives the market, because what your customers think and say about you is the most powerful force in influencing new customers to do business with you. That's the marketplace of today. Nothing compares with the power of customer word of mouth, especially on social media.

Leading a Winning Culture
Creating Your Greatest Competitive Advantage
Through Culture

If you get your culture right, it can be your key differentiator. The most valuable assets a company can have are great employees who love to come to work every day, and great potential employees who want to work for you. You can't "not" have a culture. The question is whether your culture is intentional, by design, and strengthened by leadership each and every day.

Learn real world lessons from Joe's work with market leading companies that have also been recognized nationally as "best places to work."